Last Lake

REGINALD GIBBONS

Last Lake

THE UNIVERSITY OF CHICAGO PRESS

Chicago and London

REGINALD GIBBONS is a Frances Hooper Professor of Arts and Humanities at Northwestern University. Gibbons is a poet, novelist, essayist, editor, and translator, and his many books include translations of Sophocles, Euripides, and modern Spanish and Mexican poets; the novel *Sweetbitter* and a forthcoming collection of short stories; the critical study *How Poems Think*; and nine books of poems, among them the National Book Award finalist *Creatures of a Day* and *Slow Trains Overhead: Chicago Poems and Stories*.

The University of Chicago Press, Chicago 60637
The University of Chicago Press, Ltd., London
© 2016 by The University of Chicago
All rights reserved. Published 2016.
Printed in the United States of America

25 24 23 22 21 20 19 18 17 16   1 2 3 4 5

ISBN-13: 978-0-226-41745-5 (paper)
ISBN-13: 978-0-226-41759-2 (e-book)
DOI: 10.7208/chicago/9780226417592.001.0001

Library of Congress Cataloging-in-Publication Data
Names: Gibbons, Reginald, author.
Title: Last lake / Reginald Gibbons.
Other titles: Phoenix poets.
Description: Chicago : The University of Chicago Press, 2016. | Series: Phoenix poets
Identifiers: LCCN 2016018416 | ISBN 9780226417455 (pbk. : alk. paper) | ISBN 9780226417592 (e-book)
Classification: LCC PS3557.I1392 L37 2016 | DDC 811/.54—dc23 LC record available at https://lccn.loc.gov/2016018416

♾ This paper meets the requirements of ANSI/NISO Z39.48-1992 (Permanence of Paper).

For my beloved C.

CONTENTS

ACKNOWLEDGMENTS

The author thanks the editors of the following publications in which these poems first appeared:

Academy of American Poets Poem-a-Day: "To the futile sound"
    (as "After Mandelshtam")
MAKE Literary Magazine (makemag.com): "A Veteran"
Ploughshares: "Canasta"
Plume: "I remember that," "In the rainy sub-," and *"(Persephonē)"*
Poetry: "The cranium dome," "Poor old page-earth—sized," "In dusk-lit ways, spell," and "'For your sweet joy, take"
A Public Space: "Gods never were. And"

"On Self and Soul" appeared in *Nation and World, Church and God: The Legacy of Garry Wills*, ed. Kenneth L. Vaux and Melanie Baffes (Evanston: Northwestern University Press, 2014).

One

A NEIGHBORHOOD IN CHICAGO

from a line of Gwendolyn Brooks

In its last halogen hours,
         the evening forgives the alley-
                  ways . . . wherein,

Every June morning, again,
         here are new leaves, viridian.
                  They'll come to,

Tremble toward the brightening.
         Instruments without musicians,
                  they will play

A silence, soothing last night's
         bruised pianos and exhausted
                  horns. For your

instruction, each meager leaf,
         shaped like, more intricate than, a
                  violin,

accompanies rats and moths
         into the dawn, and a cougar,
                  hiding, with

wounded eye, a torn paw: in
         halogen night, no escape—but
                  there's luck, grace.

MEMORIAL DAY
after Walt Whitman

A last formality is
running late, as a life can't,
this hot day. The final
ethereal glow of
the sun seems to come up from
underfoot in this parkland
of polysyllabic death.

These deep graves, two this time,
neatly cut into the earth,
await the arrivals,
and two adjacent heaps of
damp fertile glebe are half
blanketed by reticent
dark tarpaulins. After
the full moon's first moments of
horizon-magnified
fact and risen largesse, it
has contracted as our
heaven has passed it by and now
it floats above the crowns
of the inky trees and
well beyond bare roofs. It has
always been an entity
born dead—not a phantom, as
must be this son, a muddy

part of whom soared from cratered
waste lands far away before
landing here, and also
this veteran father,
whose heart staggered into
an ER and failed after
he heard what circumstance
had done to his one boy.

No horses—hearses, the first
two cars. A corps of six men—
they bear the heavy coffined
corpse of the father toward his
very small opening in
the planet; and six more
envoys of duty, with
much-practiced attentiveness,
slow-step the light son, an
imperfect cadaver with
handles, to his own last place.
White gloves lift up the draped
famed cloth, super-striped and
starry, from the younger
casket, fold it just so—
hands with hands over hands
in ritual honor,
a ceremony neither
of mystical creed nor
of doubter's midnights—then
they advance it to the one
who remains. She's looking

away from her burials,
down at the blades of moon grass.
She feels no great gut blows
from startled convulsive
big drums that shake the spirits
of mourners, nor any
whirring of equally
perilous small drums that
might reduce the silence.
The son is submitted as
lifeless organism to
dirt; the father's remains
descend into his pit
alongside, likewise on
tightly held ropes men slowly
let slip. (In foremost ranks of
a final unbecoming
these two fell alike.) The
ropes snake back up into
what's left of natural light—
remainder of the ancient
calculus of day and night.
From a boom box ten paces
away, the familiar
bugled notes say that the
journey of these remains
is done. Even if no grief
shadows the bugler, bugles
do sound it, word it—that
unacceptable sentence
of slow notes.

Distant, on
overtime, respectful, yet
much too near, a stranger
waits to start up a backhoe.
On such occasions, after
courage of soldiers or
folly of command or cold
wrong purposes among
patriarchs, lords, kings, and freed
madness in red valleys,
mountains, cities, villages,
in schools, shrines, sheds, beds, mud-brick
hearts, we have offered up our
mortally wounded, un-
comprehending remembrance.
We look down or away
and notice the impassive
grass under our bloody weight.

BELIEF

The lovely Director who
led us with her feathered hands
as she mouthed

the words we choir singers sang
to her and the families in
the pews—the

Director: a forbidding
figure, but forbidden, too,
who aroused

as she worshipped (and what she
aroused even in our own
hymnals was—

while bringing in the sheaves—damned
like drinking, chastised from the
high pulpit).

(Caesar's coin is still struck with
a dull clang: a new ruler's
greedy nose,

and preachers too need payment.
Some say wealth can prove the Word.)
Collection

bowls, wood, like dull shuttles down
slow pews wove the worshippers
together

as the choir hushed for three whole
verses and our organist,
reckless as

an angel, played her own ex-
uberant variations
on our self-

punishing themes. And with her
arms held up, the Director,
eyes big, brows

raised—she too, under Sunday
clothes, in her worshipful and
as far as

I could see voluptuous
Christian body—she had some
undaunted

gifted innocence in her
physical being, nothing
sordid, as

Paul said, and yet *"Listen to
me!"*: commandments and righteous
assertions,

bringing in those sheaves, condemned
all that was against holy
laws, against

the holy Judge. Body was
anathematized in the
body of

worship. "Just as I am," just
as I will be, I hear shrill
weak voices,

the plaintive congregation,
where, joined by no one, I don't
believe it.

On Thursdays our practice at
sweeter singing, and Sundays
the brimstone,

the self-abasing desire
to be unworthy, and the
gratitude

for our misery and fear.
Or at least uneasiness.
Outside, sin

in hot streets, ditches, hot shade
or cold rain; and moccasins,
copperheads,

rattlers, once a coral snake,
even Satanish-seeming
hog-nose snakes

we had caught, when younger, to
scare others at school, or pet
blood-squirting

baby horny toads—I'd tie
one by a length of mother's
thread to a

shirt button and this tiny
wide lizard'd stand on my
shoulder all

morning, a mascot from what
they said was hell if it was
related

to snakes . . . but no threat of blood
from its eyes, it asked for just
a moment's

taming (you stroked its belly)—
all those denizens of the
pagan earth,

so much just what they are, and
easier on it than we
because earth

was theirs, not ours, even then,
"when the dew was still on the"
phrases. And

the voice we heard, word by word,
and literal, rose by rose,
to fit us

for God's heaven, said *"Believe!"*
(It's here, it's all still with me!)
Did all the

fathers kill snakes? Or was cold
Satan turned into a snake
(like Cadmus

and beautiful Harmony)
so that we'd fear, hate, kill him?
(Cadmus and

gorgeous Harmony were not,
except to Dionysos
himself, true

evil.) And our tired, red-haired
Director, twelve years older
than I, the

tenor boy—or who *was* that
in the back row who had learned
that Paul spoke

Greek and wrote that it's better
to marry than to burn and
ache and burn? . . .

The Director! While her hands
were hovering in the breath
of singers,

her body, too, what a friend
we had in her, her music-
mastering

impatience. She tightened us
into the sound of us as
a choir—fire

in our shrill harmonies, we
gave her our will and shall, but
we never

came up to the morals of
the music—great choral works
or dreck. We

half wrecked half of it, achieved
scant holy worship but did
audition

for it honestly. I was
burning then, mere creature, not
wanting to be saved from fire—
not her fire.

LAST LAKE

That cold time before, she and I could
still drink the clear river water—
reaching a tin cup over the side of the canoe.
The next year, where we put in,
people were talking of giardia,
and two days out, we paddled by a whole moose carcass
left in the water the previous autumn to rot—
hunters from elsewhere had taken only the head.
Straining to beat the dark under a low sun still hot,
we were moving upstream on
the hushed waterway,
we turned into an unnamed tributary
then into another, wishing
we had learned in some village a thousand years
before our birth a song
for our paddle strokes that we could have
sung back softly to the rippling current
that was whispering to us—
she in the bow, me in the stern,
a week's supplies between us.
To an osprey we were more and more
inconvenient as we approached flashing
reflections from our paddles.
We wished not to annoy it but needed to go on.
It leapt up from a bare eighty-foot pine top
and flew upriver to another high branch

that sagged under it, and it folded its great
black-wristed wings again
and again stared sharply down its late day,
watching for a fish. But again we ruined
its chances, apologizing as we paddled toward it.
Forced to three such stages of retreat,
it up and winged over us
away to another river it knew.
All of us have never stopped building and becoming
the things that no osprey can get over.

In the thick woods on the up-sloping bank,
a steep narrow beaver slide—a young bear coming down it
scoots into sight on its behind
then sees us so near that it thrashes the underbrush
as it spins around and escapes
back up the bank fast.

In four days we made three portages.
All that heavy human stuff that we carried—
loads of it and the cooler
and then the empty heavy canoe.
Drank something very cold after each time,
having started with a block of ice so big
only one beer, one soda, and the bacon would fit beside it.

We arrived at a wide reach of tall wild rice
standing two feet high above the water
with a few grains at the top of each stalk,
rich wildflower green,
and this water is so slow

and shallow it looks still to us—a side-pond filled
with the flourishing rice. Yet there's
one opening, five or six inches wide, among the crowding stems,
and she and I turn into it and see that this too is a tributary,
and we head up what will be, wherever it leads,
our last leg of the day,
a meandering water path through the green,
leading toward wherever this tiniest of currents comes from.

We keep the nose of the canoe in
that narrow snaking channel
and in twenty minutes of slow quiet strokes, pushing down as
gently as we can among the rice stems,
where our sliding plastic and aluminum paddles
hiss against the stems then
bubble the water, we reach the source,
almost a secret place, a tiny lake,
a last one, where no one
can hike in or make a ruckus with a motorboat—
a pair of loons are in the water, as antediluvian
as everything else. A good sign. It's late,
even at this high latitude the summer sun
is almost at the treetops,
we stow our paddles and we sit
still in the still canoe for a moment.
We pick up our rods, adjust the line, reach back,
and cast the lures in two long arcs, the little splash
sounds far away, and soon we hook
two pike, release the smaller one,
then paddle to shore at a great flat rock and she stands
and steps out of the bow, gets hold of the canoe,

then I stand and step forward and onto the rock, we both
haul the canoe halfway out, and as we do,
one long dull word comes from the keel.

We get the tent up, toss sleeping bags and packs inside,
set the lantern in it, zip the mesh door shut,
gather dry wood, build a fire.
She fillets the pike, lays it crackling in the frying pan,
I fling the remains
out into the water, crawfish come eat them.

Dark trees around this lake, almost a circle
maybe two hundred feet wide,
have repeated every sound
we've made, but as question.
From the cooler we retrieve the last beer
and last soda and we drain out the last melt
of what had been our block of ice.
Five days since we put in.
From here we'll just work at it,
without the leisure of camp mornings,
and we'll paddle back downstream in two.

Somewhere inside the low branch-shadows
of a tree that might be thinking
about the end of its long bright sun-time,
a hermit thrush offers everything it has
of notes and trills, singing about Now, Now, Now,
within the thick-grown,
dark blue-green trees,
almost black, that stand around the lake

leaning at it a little, and the thrush
is an imagination, or one of them,
in the woods, one mood of the woods,
of a many-mindedness.

Then the thrush goes quiet. It requires
no such magnificence of us.

Fried pike and canned green beans for dinner,
you remember something from when we met,
the evening's a memorial for whatever we want
to put in it. Or a promise.
It seems eternal, and the frying pan gets scoured and turned
upside down on the rock,
and we hang the food duffle high up between two trees,
we wash a little in the cold little lake,
everything's taken care of, the fire dies down,
last sparks fly and float up when she toes it,
and suddenly the mosquitoes are on us like rain,
it's their moment now,
and we hurry into the tent—the only haste
we have needed all day.

One of the loons
cries through the last of the twilight
with what would be grief if we, not it,
were to make that sound. But it's not.
Then—dimly through the thin
nylon of the tent and fly
come wavering pale green veils of light
high in the north, moving like a being.

For a while we watch through the mesh
this biggest thing that the human eye can get a sense of.

I didn't say, but will now, that beyond
our broad, flat, tilted rock, in the thin dirt
where we staked the tent,
there was wild mint, and on the rock itself
we found a ring of small stones already arranged
to contain a campfire.
When native men canoe in,
the one in the bow will turn around and sit backwards,
and they both catch the tall stems of the wild rice,
bend them down across the canoe, and with a stick
they gently knock the ripe grains off the tops of them
into the canoe, and reach another armful in,
and brush that one and another
and paddle a stroke
and do it again and again and again,
working the rice slowly, for this is slow work.

When I think of all this now I have to stop
what I'm doing and saying in the midst
of all the talk, I have to stop
hearing all the mechanical and emotional noise
around me, mine, too—behind my eyes
I feel such pressure of catastrophe and awe.

CANASTA

Houston, 1953

Masses of one un-housed
household added to another, all abandoned and made
to abandon their names. A non-colonnade
of gray clods. An un-quadrangle
of neo-rational obliteration. An arcade
of ashes. Ditch-buried
hordes of kin left akimbo, a strangled
necropolis on the verge of the farthest acres of the settled
precincts of our planet—or maybe at the corner angle
of the poisoned field
of remembrance, only one little creaking shed.
And in the low gray corner inside, a weak tangle
of the last echoes of a last word
that ever was uttered to a beloved child,
or of that child's reply. "I know how to play," I said

to my grandmother, I lied—
so wanting to be included, and interrupting her card
game in America—the card table, the discard,
the talk in their languages, the tea—no more than a decade
after all that hate-whipped
grief without a shroud.
Her three card-playing women friends, as displaced
as she, did not (I remember this) like to be interrupted.
It might be too much for me to say I understand
that what they did,

their canasta and bridge, their mahjong, they did
so as, even then, not to be destroyed.
And they went out together, too—converged
with fellow Theosophists and singers and even tramped
off in pants to a mossy, snakey wood
to see a migrating bird.

If, as I stood near the card game, my grandmother reached
and touched my head—
I'm saying: if she did. I don't remember that she did.

Her own youngest son had gone all the way back there to be killed
in that war. If touch me she did,
it might have been because I, her blood-
descendant but knowing nothing, could
not have restored
to her for one second—
even if unwittingly I could have touched
her with the grace of a small child—
I could not have restored
"one iota," as she used to say, of the world
that had been obliterated, world
she never once mentioned.

ON SELF AND SOUL

Variations on the poem by W. B. Yeats
for Garry Wills

I.

The night's a metonym
       For ancestral steppes, where the oldest words made song.

       On starless nights, cold-clouded, it's not wrong
To invite imagination to respond;
And "self" or "soul" ponder what has been.

Each with a share of love, regret, and fear,
That turn us toward, or to ward off, what's broken,
We stand on an oaken, crumbling stair,
Must choose to climb or to descend,
To escape or rescue, to want an end
Or a beginning: we're wandering and frail, impure.

2.

A ploughman leans his everything—
His tattered laugh, his battering toil—
Onto the centuries, as the mule,
Without a soul, pulls blindly on and cannot sing.

What's the good of trying to escape
If always there is more to furrow and to furrow?
In obligation or a ditch, in joy or sorrow,
We too again live all that's human—asleep

And awake. Each day's a shard of looking glass:
Showing us, proud beggars,
To ourselves, flashing a glimpse of what it figures
Among the broad earth's blessings and its rigors.

3. (BRIGHT CANDLELIGHT)

Waving his saber, a rider takes porch steps with uproar
And clatter, steel-shod hooves on wood,
He must lean down to enter on his horse, and spurs it hard,
Then standing in his stirrups with groaning swing
He cuts down the glowing chandelier.

It crashes, bleeds out slowly—like a man, not a thing—
          Not in a way that one could stanch.
Outside, a kestrel on a branch,
          At rest, digesting a green lizard.

Horses won't go down steps. In the vestibule
What had been wondrously handmade
By worn-out men, dark-skinned, lies shattered
Underfoot. The blade
Is sheathed; the rider has to get the horse and his soul
          Out, clear of hazard.

And Lincoln studies a map, goes inch by inch.

4.

The question isn't whether we should be;
To think it is, you'd have to credit heaven.
(Thoughtless stars; a horse on antebellum stairs;
The airs of an ovenbird engraven
On the green hush of a dark tree,
Or the rescue of forgotten prisoners—
All these discredit plausibility.
What's plausible? Not a millionth part of nature;
Nor a million aspects of the human guise;
Neither malicious eyes of prehistoric dragonflies
Nor the forgiving gaze of Rembrandt, the etcher.)

5.

The plenitude of what is is the diet of the mind.

Go back six thousand winters—
In middens disinterred, naked to the air,
Are bones of beavers, mammoths, fish, reindeer,
Of cattle, horses, boars, and bears.

Once in a while, of humankind.

And in harm's way, an excavated cemetery, too—
Reopened wound that even a breeze makes ache,
A breathless ditch made sacred for a sky-god's sake:
Bronze blades, tooth beads, and charms against the bugaboo—

The evil eye. Here are male skeletons in which
Precise projectile points are still stuck fast in ribs,
Spines, necks; here are some heads that other tribes,
Using wood clubs, inscribed with a live hole in each.

Gods of the sky, come see again the Mesolithic tombs
Dedicated to you, where even battle-dogs were buried
With warrior grave-goods—fully as dead and wearied
As men, but honored like them too with beads and plumes.

War-horses of the steppes. (Of course—for that's
How human force made more of its force.) And consecrated
By ritual sacrifice, their flesh fat-feasted the fated
Survivors who built death-realm habitats,

Used symbolic stuff to remind the gods of men; to bind
The gods to men with the prayers of a bard
And by oath, in reciprocal regard.

6.

"Soul," the word, is ancient (from Old English).
"Self," the word, is older (Indo-European).
The sound of either word can span an eon
And revivify the history of a wish.

A mortal man or woman, composed of self and soul,
Or thought and act, or guest and host.
A mortal man or woman—not a god and not a beast—

Must live a question, questioning;
Can weep with happiness; can excruciate
And nullify; or sanctify; or both. Can turn, and honoring
The dust of all creation, can create.

May dance when lame; and even mute, may sing;
And can. Can howl when well and laugh when ill,
Love when in pain, and in pain, love still.

7.

Livingness itself, neither bad nor benign,
Cannot discriminate
A kindness from a crime, and does not abate,
No matter how work hurts us, or love, or a hurricane.

Anxiously a woman rushes home, tight-lipped.
Is everyone all right? Where's my child?

Something's coming. Rescue or some other fate.
With grief, the ploughman smiles, he glances up—a sign,
That smile, as surely as his furrow is a script.
As surely as a few words, ordered in one line
Or hundreds, to say what's what,
May for a moment interrupt.

RITUAL
February 1966

A slow parade of old west enthusiasts,
camp song and hymn, came in along the winding

way where rural declined to suburban, slow
riders and wagoners passing a cow staked

to graze, some penned cattle looking vacantly
up—not in vacant lots the ancient icons

of wealth they had been in odes, prayers, and epics,
in sacrifices and customs of bride-price

or dowry. (It's good people no longer make
blood sacrifices, at gas stations and stores,

for example, and in the crunching gravel
parking lots of small churches—oh, but we do.)

And alongside the paved so-called trail super-
imposed on roads toward all the way downtown,

schoolkids and neighbors waited a long while to
see it all pass on Indo-European

wheels, the riders holding hot coffee, clinking,
clopping, calling out, slowing ordinary

traffic, waving hats, their leather tack creaking
through their historical enthusiasms—

dear old ideology of cotton and
cotton candy and steak at the arena.

Soldiers on leave, here, there, watching, and if black,
etc., only acknowledged by whites

when they were gone and were dead, and we didn't
read their so brief obituaries, didn't

notice their pressed dress uniform photos. . . . But
now the fallen and the returned were like loose

used parts from the place of their manufacture
inside everyone else's heads—figures of

our so loudly hallowed mistake. We all heard
sharply voiced, "Whoa! Whoa! Whoa!" or lashing of quirts

to move a stubborn beast on or a hiss to
force a mount step by step backwards (sound of the

dragon-snake, enemy of equids) to keep
taut the braided rope on a cow. For hours the

American caravan passed—pack horses,
too, mounts in remudas, held by hackamores;

geldings, stallions, mares, ponies; horses with no
knowledge of raids, war-chariots with savage

bridles, of ploughing, dragging logs, hauling earth
for tombs, of the shock of the blood odor of

other horses sacrificed at funerals.
Fat trail-drive horses with no epics of men

urinating in their enemies' dead mouths,
of ululating women . . .

A BOOKSHELF

In my flatland fatherland, I'll put
    one ear to the sky

or a pine or the earth, down
    on my knees I'll do it

now, at home, inside my room
    of a thousand human

summits still vibrating so very
    quietly on paper

and shelves, both made of trees,
    each book like

a generation of cicadas, each one
    the size of the letter

a: I hear "I've hung a shield from Thrace
    in Athena's Parthenon"

(some character is rasping at me
    from his single

page among the fragments of lost
    tragedies; he

means he cannot serve as
    a soldier

any longer), "let my spear
    lie dead, let

spiders weave tangles around it"
    (he whispers

loudly), "may I live in peace through
    my gray years,

may I sing poems, may I unroll the voices
    in the scrolls."

DIVERGENCE

of the mail,
the return portion's 'Keep For'
left lying around—
readies for the poem (divergent response).

The arriving envelope
opens space on its back
for incoming,
anything at hand for anything
to write on.
—Ed Roberson

—

(*Yosemite*)

And I, on the back of the rhetoric
inside the envelope that's still
imploring me even after being

eviscerated with a dull ebony
blade and annoyed fingers . . .
on yet another piece of mail,

I mean, that's pale and available to
a pencil, I stub my new-
joined words, only half

heard even by me, the one
who writes them, I line
them up and down, they're

not yet themselves as they
might be, may be, may
never be, but already

they could fly if I threw
this dead envelope clean
across the deep cold vertigo—

from my rolling chair on
the overhang of Glacier
Point to the uneven top
of El Capitán: my table.

———

With binoculars I watch
the red fox on the postage stamp

venture herself across new
meadow snow three thousand feet

below me, her minute blue
tracks written on the flat

two dimensions of the
white she marks, at the foot

of a stilled leviathan of stone
that had leaned back, eons ago,

awaiting such scripts as hers,
which it would never read.

——— ——— ——— ——— ———

(*Scafell Pike*)

Land-shapes of night, no one to be seen,
   when Dorothy
Wordsworth's remote brother
   left their
small cottage at midnight,

went striding for miles up the road under
   "huge peaks,
black and huge," in the moonlight
   and quiet
of lower hills and lakes. Subsiding

to his knees at a crest, William put
   his impatient
appetite for news sideways against the hard
   earth and listened for
faint rumbling wagon wheels and

horses' hooves—his mail and his
        London newspaper.
The driver in no hurry. In
        the scratchy weft
of young William's woolen collar

must have been hairs from his
        own head and
a few of his sister's, and odors of
        the close cottage
that the sweet rural air of night

now wafts away from him. . . .
        In his trouser
cuffs and socks: spores, grains
        of pollen,
dirt from muddy up and down

rambles off the paths, from
        high sheep fields
where he's been strenuously diverging
        from main roads
and everybody else's ways of

writing a poem. Probably it
        wasn't Dorothy
who so craved the latest word.
        William's standing
up again, he leans toward

the recent past, awaits the
      heavy wagon
rolling post by post, he might walk
      back, unwilling to
wait longer. We ourselves aren't

mountains more than patient
      enough for
the erosion of a few hours. We're not
      quiet. And our mail,
our news, our language junk,

      junk language—
the blank back of it's ready
      for more than
we'll ever imagine writing or reading.
      We don't launch
ourselves, all of us, into enough
      divergence.

A VETERAN

My father came down not killed
from among others, killers or killed,
for whom he'd worn a uniform,
and he lived a long afterward,

a steady man on the flattest of plains.
I called after him many times, surprised
when I heard the catch in my own voice.
He didn't know how to find the solace

of listening to someone else speak of
what he'd seen and survived.
He himself closed his own
mouth against his own words.

In the wrong sequence, his spirit,
then his mind, and last his body
crossed over that infamous, peat-inky,
metaphorical water that has no far shore.

I think he was carried like a leaf
in currents so gentle that a duckling,
had it been alive, could have braved them,
but too strong for a leaf. And saturated

with minerals that steadily replaced
organic cells, the water turned my father,
an ex-soldier, to leaf-delicate stone inscribed
with the axioms of countless veins.

Two

DARK HONEY

from and for Osip Mandelshtam (1891–1938)

I.

In the rainy sub-
tropics of my child-
hood, horse latitudes
of sleep, of handmade
wishes, I would try
to dream of snow-fields.
But they failed to be-
come real as I lay
on my sweaty sheet
after we'd all been
outside late among
the invisible
heat-giants trampling
the unbreathable
dusk. The sun, gone down
behind the china-
berry trees of our
gunman back neighbor,
had left on the mute
bulging stratosphere
its faint pledge never
to fail us. I wished
and imagined it
would fail us just once,

give me a chance, I'd
take our one horse, ride
in the broad midday
darkness far away.

2.

I remember that
our hell-hot pear tree,
so southerly, so
dark-green-minded, held
with a negative
theology—took
up that logic, so
logy with summer
Logos that it bore
small fruit which refused
to ripen; if plucked
from those green anti-
fundamentalist
branches, it cooked up
into a grainy
pear-pap tasting of
nothing, not even
threats or promises.
Surely not Eden.

3.

Gods never were. And
July's no temple.
Only the Greeks thought
of Muses. Yet some
people fervently
believed—as now; felt
favored—just as now,
after tornados
or hurricane winds
that they, although not
others, have survived. . . .
July light in the
whole sky is holy,
never the less so,
somehow: when birds fly
they prove sky's always
inviolable,
never ever cut
once—even though it's
wounded and sick. The
word "holy" resounds
still, it tried to be
a verb but could not,
it reverberates
from beyond disturbed
horizons where it
still means something good.

4.

In seaside autumn,
in a port city,
silent in a cab
at a red-eyed light.
Then up wheeled the hand-
trundled chariot
of an invalid
ex-sailor—Navy-
blue ship cap on his
concussed endurance.
The gold-braid script said
U. S. S. Something,
to the cabbie he
said, "Captain," and his
captain gave him coins;
he said, "Thank you, Sir."
This survivor then
in emotional
slow motion rolled past
my rolled-down window
on his way to find
a better man of
good wishes than I,
but he—trim, somber,
calm, with cut-off legs,
café-con-leche
skin, and almond eyes,
this man I had been
looking at for a

very long instant—
did crisply salute
me, leaning toward me,
grave and wry, judging.

5. *(THE BIG RIVER)*

Beside the railway
weedy with burdock,
the summer platform
(Stay Behind Line!), a
bright yellow footstool
awaiting the next
train. . . . Let's step onto
it then far beyond
these tracks to the deck
of that green tugboat
that's preemptively
heading upriver
against one-wayness;
another yellow
step flies us up to
the wing of the small
airplane overhead,
and from there we can
vault at an angle
to what no compass
shows, to indirect
dimensions we can
not know, yet we do.

6.

The skull has evolved
all its forehead-breadth,
temple to Temple,
is amused by its
own sutures, features,
futures. Omniscient,
its cupola gleams,
it froths with ideas,
dreams of itself—a
chalice (by some, used
as such) beyond all
chalices, mother-
land of mother tongues,
father of godhood,
cap of happiness
and horror, a star-
thinking exemplar.

7.

(I sense by its im-
perceptible touch
that from the farthest
remove of the known
universe a dazed
ray too weak to be
seen is standing on
my closed rhyming eyes.

I hear the whisper
of the magnetic
attraction between
two blood-warm iron-ore
verbs, the palpable
pebbly sound of them.)

8.

The cranium dome
hangs from its own thread
of virtual pale
light, conceiving its
exercises of
inventiveness, its
associative
super-supremo-
conductivity,
its color wheel of
lucid and lulu,
its murk and murder,
worthy and woo-woo
heterodoxy,
its Zeno, its Zeus,
its Dante, its Te
Deums and freak shows,
frescoes, twine theory,
money, bread, bricks, wine,
sex, six-syllable
abstractions, axes
and genetic in-
genuity of
custom, including
kisses, verbs, and the
vertical graves of
men buried upside
down without their heads.

9.

Poor old page-earth—sized,
cut, scraped, ink-scribed or
impressed, or ploughed with
mulish impulses,
illuminated
by thought brightly or
obscured, or both; in
some times revered, in
some destroyed, or both.
I've asked myself and
I am sure I do
not believe we can
move a pencil through
a white field, pulled by
a team of upside-
down ox-head letter
*A*s, and in real fact
furrow it. But with
tongue I snick the team.

10.

Mandelshtam's Greek bees
turn the honey back
into sun. We too
head toward reverses:
leaves transforming their
orange into green.
Don't shores erode the
seas, don't riverbanks
flow upstream, aren't wounds
caused by blood, don't stars
produce the night, and
doesn't extinction
vivify the new-
born, don't dreams produce
our dulled sleeplessness . . .

II.

Even on remote
mountaintops time knows
no justice and time
will survive and time
has begun to move
not in terse seasons
but in a long mood,
multi-millennial,
that nothing we'll know
will ever reverse.
Sleeping might seem best.
In natural night-
mares we will reason
we should establish
a funeral home
for deceased species.

12.

This craft of the ear's
not seen as so fine
or hard to learn as
it was. Even so,
what's most difficult
is the cruel weight of
what's waiting to be
put in a poem and
can't make its way in
if the maker can't
sense it, can't wish to
sense it, can't listen.

13.

Rivers of gasping
carburetors stream
past our voting booths
down boulevards of
crystal lipstick con-
fessionals, of face
polish, of new jeans—
the blue icons of
our not having two
legs to not stand on.
And so? And so what?
Out double mirror
doors to glass-bottom
avenues we go,
confessing our all
to electrons. We
walk our appetites
on spangly leashes,
leg our way through town,
text past the strong arms
of shooters and clowns.
And where are our stars?
Weren't they supposed
to show? Where, the dog-
toothed financiers, the
magistrates of blood
accounts, the success-
fully elected?—
We don't see them or

their art collections
and car-collector
off-shore cash stashes,
gated clinics, their
pious jets, assault
weepings, and über-
politicking till
it's too late to get
out of their damned and
indemnified way
when they pocket us
as they free-fall by.

14. (BUT . . .)

I'm looking for the
old pianos that
trembled when blind hands
sped up and down wild
runs impeccably
and ears half-squinted
at melodies. Lots
of that bent black wood
curved all the way back
to wolves in snow that
would sing, maybe weep,
to improvising
flocks of chickadees,
kinglets, titmice, and
warblers squeezing their
high notes . . . choruses
of abiding. . . . Shall
we listen to what
a songstress was at
midnight, to those old
pianos crafted
from the same trees that
had provided for
birds a habitat—
but cut now, joined, glued,
to set the soothing
of low melodies
whose habitats could
be musical keys

in different modes, moods?
Be there to hear her—
woman at the black-
and-white chords and blue
notes, she will begin,
she will bring it in
for us one more time.

15.

It's so wisely that
the dome of Hagia
Sophia hangs from
Heaven on gold chain,
and that the nib, bright
platinum of the
Greek mountain home of
poetry, floats up-
ward higher than snow
clouds and spills the ink-
well of song into
rivers, lakes, harbors,
straits—the filled footprints
of winter beliefs,
summer convictions,
pleasure and pain that's
immeasurably
old . . . and neither/nor
gold, lead; true, untrue. . . .

16.

To the futile sound
of midnight church bells,
out back someone is
rinsing her thoughts in
unfathomable
universal sky—
a cold faint glowing.
As always stars glint
white as salt on the
blade of an old axe.
Like mica in soil.
The rain barrel's full,
there's ice in its mouth.
Smash the ice—comets
and stars melt away
like salt, the water
darkens, and the earth
on which the barrel
stands is transparent
underfoot, and there
too are galaxies,
ghost-pale, silent in
the seven-thousand-
odd chambers of our
inhuman being.

17. (O. M.)

Not forgotten now,
the poet doomed then
might be imagined
to murmur something:
"Tongue gone; deaf; with few
words and with grief-struck
lungs, black raspberries
for wasp-eyes. And I'm
not unique! . . . and am.
I don't sing—I'm some
thing that barely breathes.
Blocking each ear, a
mountain. Around me,
in me, numbed nouns that
can't hear each other . . .
but I hear them. They're
a one-winged song that
hums down in the moss
and chants in green shade,
solos in prison.
A choir of one voice
on horseback, hillback.

History is the
beast too big for us
to imagine, its
back's a mountain of
trash, and that's where I
sprawl, and my ragged

two-winged coat's starving,
there's only a word
or two I can warm
my fists with, a last
image or two in
the mind of the wind."

18.

Can't keep up with fierce
accelerating
honey-sweet songs that
call to so much in
me, can't feel it all
fast enough, half can't
breathe when I try to.
The scale of the real
is this: each life so
vast but easy as
a blossom to crush.
Pavilions of out-
flying nebulae,
silver galaxies
of cold candlewax,
hang suspended like
whole cities stolen
from earth and floating
only a thousand
miles up.

    (Oh that like-
ness is as feeble
as an amoeba.)

What of the epic-
length slipping of all
the human tongues that
have ever spoken?

Didn't they always
say more than was meant.
What of the silent
deafening water-
fall of all our long-
ing since forever?
And in the clumps of
fire yellow on the
busy-body back
legs of a bumble
bee, each single grain
of pollen a world!
And in the best of
the thousand cities
on each grain, someone's
chanting another
Iliad . . .
     "Sing, Goddess . . .

19. *(PERSEPHONĒ)*

The Cretan sky's too
bright for human eyes,
near the empty road
on gust-beaten high-
lands, an old stone wind-
mill, abandoned, with-
out vanes, defends, like
a ghost fortress of
memory, all the
depopulated
myths and history
here and in the sea—
gone into the past
tense that time perfects.

Here's a chance for us:
we can elude the
way our usual
hour's saturated
by so much we did
not want to be ours.

The black opening
of a missing door
calls us in. For a
buzzing moment we
see very little.
Dark scent of honey—
faint, from acacia

and flowering thyme.
Thin gold blades of sky
piercing gaps of lost
mortar; a bee swarm,
growling, drowsy, is
swaying in the air,
far from sweet sources,
swarm of a goddess—
deathless refugee,
one who long ago
abandoned her bees—
interhovering,
droning with choral
voice their *sephonay*,
sephonay. Confused
with them, we under-
stand them—still mourning
their lost one, their lost
all. And who or what
will come to warrant
her existence now?
Word-sounds that want to
think their way forward,
interweaving and
hovering, humming,
almost resolve in
our ears. The windmill,
abyss of wonder
filled with our dizzy
longing to see, to
have back—*sephonay!*—

life-wise, those we have
lost, those we will lose.
(But we are alive—
let me kiss you now.)

20.

Against the paper-
pale day, winter twigs
devise K, F, X,
M, H, V, N, or
maybe Π (pi), Σ (sigma),
Z (zeta), Ψ (upsilon),
Λ (lambda), and their like.
No fate nor any
clerk has made these forms.
Yet trees asleep in
winter, not saying
or meaning, can be
alphabetical.
They don't need us to
read them; it's them we
needed, long ago,
to learn how to read.

21.

The memory of
her slanting brows like
wings flew her to him
from where she had gone—
completely and for
all time. Thrilling, as
always it was, and
fleeting: her figure
in close fog moved past
his touch. With intent
neither profane nor
even believing,
he blurted out, "God!"

Like an enormous
bird, this Name, which he
could not expunge from
his being, leapt out
of him, took wing, knocked
him down crumbling flights
of regret. Where she
had gone, the bird went
too. Now his ribs clacked,
having become an
empty cage for some
thing that has no . . .

22.

Well, good-bye! Wishing
you all the best! from
our soup kitchens, our
churches, our border
checkpoints, our beds and
riverbeds, our home
and military
theaters, our press rooms,
classrooms, and bliss rooms,
our refugee camps,
our empathy dumps,
our Wi-Fi hot spots,
our broadband pisspots,
western disunions,
political romps,
and other cash zones!
Good-bye to all you
multiple millions
murdered everywhere,
killed everywhen, who
then trudged your weary
atomic way to
catatonic warps
of parallel worlds
(more god-fearing ones?—
where we fill our fear
up with god or god
with fear) . . . here's wishing
you and us the best!

23.

In dusk-lit ways, spell
me, tell me, little
swallow—Tuscan or
T'ang or from other
sorrow times—how with-
out feather or wing
I too can find for
myself a grave made
only of the air.

24.

"For your sweet joy, take
"from my cupped hands a
"little glittering
"of sun, a little
"honey—for this is
"what Persephonë's
"bees have commanded.

"A boat can't cast off
"if it isn't moored;
"no one can hear a
"shadow that wears fur
"boots; we can't best our
"fright in this dark wood.

"Our kisses—these are
"all that we can save,
"velvety as bees
"that die if they are
"exiled from the hive.

"They're murmuring in
"the translucent groves
"of the night; the wilds
"of mountain Greece are
"their native land; their
"diet is time, lung-
"wort, pale meadowsweet.

"For joy, please, take this
"pagan gift: this rude,
"rustling necklace of
"the bees that died, for
"these had transmuted
"honey into sun."

NOTE

"Dark Honey": Eleven of the poems in this sequence include an image or phrase (or several) from poems by Mandelshtam, drawn either from the translations I have made with Ilya Kutik or from published translations by others. Not all such images have the same imaginative or emotional valence they have in the original poems. The last poem—number 24, "For your sweet joy"—is a close translation of a complete and well-known poem by O. M.